GUIDE TO VIDEO EDITING TECHNIQUES

I0477830

Practical Tips for Engaging Visual Effects

MARCUS T. HOOKS

COPYRIGHT

TABLE OF CONTENTS

INTRODUCTION

Unleashing the Power of Video Editing

In today's digital age, video has become one of the most influential and widely consumed forms of content. From social media and marketing to film and education, video content has the power to inform, inspire, and entertain audiences worldwide. Behind every compelling video is a well-thought-out editing process, where raw footage is transformed into a cohesive, engaging, and polished story. Video editing is where the magic happens, where emotions are amplified, and stories come alive. It's both an art form and a technical skill—one that requires creativity, precision, and a deep understanding of various techniques.

Welcome to *Guide to Video Editing Techniques,* your comprehensive roadmap to mastering the art of video editing. This book is designed to guide you through the essential techniques, tools, and principles needed to edit videos with confidence and creativity. Whether you're a complete beginner looking to dive into the world of editing or an intermediate editor aiming to sharpen your skills, this book provides everything you need to take your editing abilities to the next level.

Why Video Editing Matters

At its core, video editing is about storytelling. It's the process that takes an idea or message and refines it into something that resonates with viewers. Imagine a film without dramatic cuts or a tutorial video without clear transitions; without editing, most videos would lack structure and impact. Editing determines how scenes flow, how emotions build, and how viewers experience the narrative. It's a skill that can elevate any form of content, turning even the simplest footage into something memorable.

Today, video editing skills are more valuable than ever. Social media platforms like YouTube, Instagram, and TikTok thrive on video content, and businesses, influencers, and individuals alike are constantly creating and sharing videos to connect with their audiences. With the rise of video-based marketing and entertainment, having strong editing skills can open doors to countless opportunities, from freelance work and content creation to filmmaking and digital marketing. Whether your goal is to create captivating videos for personal projects, build a professional portfolio, or start a career in media production, learning video editing is a powerful way to bring your ideas to life.

What This Book Will Teach You

Guide to Video Editing Techniques is structured to provide a clear, step-by-step approach to video editing, covering both the basics and more advanced methods. Each chapter is designed to build upon the previous one, helping you develop a well-rounded skill set. By the end of this book, you'll understand how to use editing software confidently, choose the right cuts, add visual effects, refine audio, and even colour grade your footage to create a polished, professional-looking final product.

Here's a glimpse of what you'll learn:

- **Fundamentals of Video Editing:** We'll start with the essentials, including file organization, understanding timelines, and learning the basic tools in popular editing software. You'll also get familiar with foundational editing terms and concepts, such as resolution, frame rate, and aspect ratio, which are essential for creating high-quality videos.

- **Core Techniques for Seamless Storytelling:** You'll learn how to use core editing techniques like cutting, trimming, and merging clips to create a smooth narrative flow. These are the building blocks of any successful edit, and mastering them will give you confidence in handling a wide range of projects.

- **Enhancing Visuals with Color and Effects:** To make your videos visually appealing, you'll explore color correction and color grading techniques, as well as learn how to add effects that fit the mood and style of your project. These techniques can take a standard video to the next level, adding a cinematic feel that captures viewers' attention.

- **Perfecting Sound:** Audio is just as important as visuals when it comes to effective video editing. You'll learn how to balance dialogue, add background music, and incorporate sound effects to enrich the viewer's experience. Proper audio editing can make a video feel more immersive and professional, even on a smaller scale.

- **Adding Text and Graphics:** Text and graphics are often crucial in videos, especially for tutorials, social media content, and promotional videos. This book will show you how to incorporate titles, captions, and motion graphics to communicate information clearly and creatively.

- **Advanced Techniques for Professional Edits:** As you gain confidence, we'll dive into advanced techniques, such as multi-camera editing, green screen compositing, and slow-motion effects. These methods will give your videos a polished, professional edge that stands out from the rest.

- **Exporting and Sharing Your Work:** Finally, you'll learn how to export your videos in the best format and resolution for various platforms. Sharing your work is an essential part of the process, and understanding export settings ensures that your video looks its best, whether it's on YouTube, social media, or a professional portfolio.

This book aims to not only teach you editing techniques but to help you understand why and when to use them. Video editing is about making creative choices that serve your content and captivate your audience. Each technique covered here serves a purpose, and by the end of this book, you'll know how to make decisions that enhance the story you want to tell.

Who This Book Is For

Guide to Video Editing Techniques is designed for anyone with a passion for video editing, from beginners to those with some experience who want to refine their skills. If you're new to video editing, this book will provide you with a solid foundation, taking you from the basics of software navigation to applying professional techniques confidently. For intermediate editors, this book offers deeper insights into more complex techniques, helping you push your boundaries and add a professional polish to your projects.

This book is also for creators, small business owners, aspiring filmmakers, and anyone who uses video as part of their personal or professional life. In today's digital landscape, video editing is a valuable skill for content creators, marketers, and influencers who want to connect with their audience through engaging visuals. No matter where you are on your editing journey, this book will give you the knowledge and tools you need to create impressive, high-quality videos.

The Art and Science of Editing

Video editing sits at the intersection of art and science. While technical skills are essential, the true essence of editing lies in the creative choices you make. Knowing how to use the tools is one part of the process; understanding how to create emotion, suspense, excitement, or empathy through those tools is another. Great editing is intuitive and relies on a sense of timing, rhythm, and pacing that takes practice to develop.

In this book, we'll explore both the technical and creative aspects of editing, providing you with the tools and confidence to experiment and find your unique editing style. Video editing is a journey, and while this book will teach you valuable techniques, it's your curiosity and creativity that will ultimately drive your growth as an editor. Embrace the journey, experiment fearlessly, and remember that every project is an opportunity to learn something new.

Making the Most of This Book

To get the most out of this book, I encourage you to actively apply what you learn to real projects. Start with short videos or personal projects that allow you to practice each technique. Take your time with each chapter, experiment with different approaches, and don't be afraid to make mistakes. The best way to learn video editing is by doing, so dive in, explore, and challenge yourself to apply each technique in ways that feel authentic to your style.

As you work through this book, remember that every great editor started as a beginner. Mastery comes from consistent practice, curiosity, and a willingness to grow. Allow yourself the time to build your skills, and celebrate each milestone, no matter how small. With dedication, patience, and a passion for storytelling, you'll find that video editing becomes not only a skill but a creative outlet that allows you to bring your ideas to life in powerful, visually compelling ways.

Welcome to the World of Video Editing

The world of video editing is vast, full of potential, and constantly evolving. By picking up this book, you're taking the first step toward mastering a skill that has the power to shape how stories are told and how audiences engage with content. *Guide to Video Editing Techniques* is here to support you through every step, providing you with the guidance and knowledge to become a confident, skilled, and creative video editor.

So let's get started on this journey. Embrace each chapter with enthusiasm, learn the techniques, apply them with intention, and most importantly, enjoy the process of creating. Video editing is more than just a set of skills; it's a craft, an art, and a powerful way to connect with people through storytelling. As you dive into the pages of this book, remember that every edit, every cut, and every choice you make brings you closer to mastering the art of video editing.

Welcome to the exciting world of video editing. Let's begin this journey together!

CHAPTER 1

Getting Started with Video Editing

Video editing is both an art and a technical skill, transforming raw footage into a structured, compelling narrative. It is the process of manipulating and rearranging video shots to create a final product that tells a story, conveys information, or evokes emotions in viewers. As we explore the world of video editing, it's essential to understand that editing goes beyond simply cutting and pasting clips together; it's about creating a seamless experience for viewers, one that brings out the message or mood in a captivating way.

The importance of video editing cannot be overstated in today's media-driven world. Every video we watch, from movies and TV shows to YouTube tutorials and social media clips, has undergone some form of editing. A well-edited video has the power to enhance storytelling, build suspense, clarify complex information, and even elicit emotions that resonate with audiences. By carefully choosing and arranging scenes, an editor can control the pacing, mood, and message, shaping how the audience perceives the content.

In this chapter, we'll delve into the basics of video editing, its role in media, the equipment and software you'll need, and essential concepts like resolution, aspect ratio, and frame rate. We'll also cover tips for setting up an organized workflow, ensuring you have a smooth editing process from start to finish.

Overview of Video Editing and Its Role in Media

Video editing plays a pivotal role in media production. In an age where visual content dominates, the demand for skilled video editors is higher than ever. Editing has become indispensable across a wide range of media formats, from feature films and documentaries to corporate videos and online tutorials. Let's explore the significant ways in which video editing shapes the media we consume:

- **Storytelling in Film and TV:** In films and television, editors work closely with directors to bring the script to life. They control the rhythm and flow of scenes, ensuring that the narrative unfolds in a way that engages the audience. Editors in these roles carefully select which shots to include, determining the impact of each scene on the storyline and the audience's emotional experience.

- **Creating Compelling Marketing Content:** Video marketing has exploded in popularity, with companies using videos to promote products, explain services, and build brand identity. In this setting, editors are responsible for crafting concise, visually appealing videos that convey the brand's message effectively. A well-edited marketing video can make a lasting impression on viewers, driving engagement and sales.

- **Educating and Informing Audiences:** Many online platforms, such as YouTube and educational websites, rely on video to teach skills, explain concepts, and share information. In these videos, editing helps maintain a smooth flow, ensuring that the information is easy to follow and understand. Proper editing techniques, such as using transitions and text overlays, can help emphasize key points and guide the viewer's attention.

- **Social Media and Personal Content Creation:** Social media platforms like Instagram, TikTok, and Facebook have transformed the way people create and share video content. Here, editing is often used to make short, engaging videos that capture attention quickly. Social media editing emphasizes creativity, with fast cuts, effects, and music playing a big role in attracting viewers and creating shareable content.

No matter the medium or purpose, editing allows creators to tailor their message and connect with their audience in a meaningful way. As you embark on this journey, remember that video editing gives you the power to shape stories, evoke emotions, and influence how others perceive your content.

Essential Equipment and Software Options (Basic to Professional)

Getting started with video editing doesn't require a massive investment in equipment, but having the right tools can significantly improve the quality and efficiency of your work. Here's a breakdown of essential equipment and software options, from beginner-friendly tools to professional-grade setups.

Essential Equipment for Video Editing

1. **Computer or Laptop**

   The first and most important piece of equipment for video editing is a computer with sufficient processing power. Video editing software requires considerable memory and CPU/GPU power, especially for high-definition and 4K video files. For beginners, any modern desktop or laptop with at least 8GB of RAM, a quad-core processor, and a decent graphics card will suffice. As you progress, upgrading to 16GB or 32GB of RAM and a more powerful processor can significantly speed up your editing workflow.

2. **External Storage Drives**

Video files are large, and editing projects can quickly consume your computer's storage space. External storage drives (HDD or SSD) are essential for storing your footage, project files, and final exports. Solid-state drives (SSDs) are recommended for faster data access, which speeds up file transfers and project loading times.

3. **Headphones or Studio Monitors**

Audio quality is an integral part of video editing. Good-quality headphones or studio monitors allow you to hear your audio clearly, making it easier to balance sound levels, eliminate background noise, and add sound effects. Headphones are a practical choice for beginners, but as you advance, consider investing in studio monitors for a more accurate audio experience.

4. **Editing Monitors**

A high-quality monitor provides better color accuracy, making it easier to perform color correction and grading. While not essential for beginners, dual monitors can improve productivity by allowing you to view your timeline on one screen and your footage on another.

Software Options: Basic to Professional

1. **iMovie (Mac) and Windows Movie Maker (PC)**
   For beginners, iMovie (Mac) and Windows Movie Maker (PC) are free, user-friendly options that cover the basics of video editing, including cutting, trimming, adding transitions, and simple text overlays. These programs are great for learning foundational skills before moving on to more advanced software.

2. **Adobe Premiere Pro**

Adobe Premiere Pro is one of the most popular and versatile editing programs on the market, used by professionals across various industries. Premiere Pro offers extensive features, including multi-track editing, advanced color grading, and support for various plugins. With a subscription-based model, it's accessible to both beginners and professionals, making it an excellent choice for those who want a high level of control and flexibility.

3. **Final Cut Pro X**

Exclusive to Mac users, Final Cut Pro X is known for its intuitive interface and powerful features. It provides advanced editing capabilities, such as multi-camera editing, color correction, and motion graphics. Its performance optimization for Mac hardware makes it a favorite among professional editors working on creative projects.

4. **DaVinci Resolve**

DaVinci Resolve is a robust editing platform known for its industry-leading color grading tools. It's free to download and offers a paid Studio version with extra features, making it a great choice for editors at all levels. Resolve is particularly useful for those who want to develop strong color grading skills, as its tools are some of the best available in the industry.

5. **Mobile Apps (e.g., Adobe Premiere Rush, InShot, KineMaster)**

   For those looking to edit on the go, mobile apps like Adobe Premiere Rush, InShot, and KineMaster provide surprisingly powerful features for smartphones and tablets. These apps are excellent for quick edits, social media content, and beginner projects, offering features like trimming, text overlays, and transitions.

Each of these software options offers unique advantages, so choose one that fits your budget, skill level, and project needs. As you progress in your editing journey, you may find that investing in more advanced tools is a natural next step.

Key Concepts: Resolution, Aspect Ratio, Frame Rate

Understanding technical terms is crucial for producing high-quality videos. Three key concepts that every video editor should understand are resolution, aspect ratio, and frame rate.

1. **Resolution**

   Resolution refers to the number of pixels in each frame of your video, typically measured by width and height (e.g., 1920 x 1080 pixels for Full HD).

Higher resolution means more detail and clarity, but also larger file sizes. Common resolutions include:

- **720p (HD):** Basic high-definition quality, suitable for smaller screens.
- **1080p (Full HD):** Standard for most online content, providing excellent quality for various devices.
- **4K (Ultra HD):** High resolution, offering exceptional detail, popular for high-end production and streaming.

2. **Aspect Ratio**

Aspect ratio is the proportional relationship between the width and height of your video frame. The aspect ratio affects how the video appears on different screens. Common aspect ratios include:

- **16:9:** Widely used for most online platforms and standard television.
- **4:3:** Classic TV format, now less common.
- **1:1:** Square format popular on social media platforms like Instagram.
- **9:16:** Vertical video format used for Instagram Stories, TikTok, and Snapchat.

3. **Frame Rate**

    Frame rate, measured in frames per second (fps), determines how many individual frames are displayed each second. It affects the smoothness of motion in your video:

- **24 fps:** Standard frame rate for cinematic content.
- **30 fps:** Common for television and online video.
- **60 fps and above:** Used for sports and action scenes, as it captures smoother motion.

Understanding these concepts allows you to make informed choices, ensuring that your video is compatible with the platform and audience's viewing preferences.

Tips for Setting Up an Organized Workflow

A well-organized workflow is essential for efficient video editing, allowing you to manage files, timelines, and edits without becoming overwhelmed. Here are some tips to help you set up a smooth, organized editing workflow:

1. **Create a Folder Structure**

    Start by creating a structured folder for each project. Common folders might include "Raw Footage," "Audio," "Graphics," and "Exports." Clear organization prevents lost files and makes it easy to find what you need as you work.

2. **Rename Your Files**

Rename your files descriptively. Instead of "clip1.mov," use names like "Interview_John_Scene1.mov" for easy identification.

3. **Use Editing Software Bins**

Most editing software allows you to create "bins" or folders within the project, making it easier to sort footage, audio, and other elements within your workspace.

4. **Save Frequently**

Video editing software can be intensive on your computer's resources, making crashes possible. Save your work frequently, and consider creating backup copies as you progress.

5. **Use a Consistent Naming Convention**

Develop a naming convention for your project files, such as including the date and version number (e.g., "ProjectName_V1_2023"). Consistency in naming helps with organization and prevents accidental overwriting of files.

With these foundational principles, equipment options, technical concepts, and workflow tips in place, you're now equipped to embark on your video editing journey. This chapter has set the stage, offering an introduction to the world of video editing and providing the practical knowledge you need to begin confidently.

As you move forward, remember that each video you create is an opportunity to refine your skills, experiment with techniques, and bring your unique storytelling style to life.

CHAPTER 2

Understanding the Basics of Editing Software

Video editing software is the heart of any editing project, enabling you to transform raw footage into a polished, engaging story. With the right software, you have the tools to cut, merge, enhance, and refine video clips, creating a final product that aligns with your vision. Understanding the essentials of video editing software, its features, and workflow is crucial for both beginners and experienced editors. Each software offers unique strengths, and this chapter will guide you through popular options, key tools, and practical steps for getting started.

In this chapter, we'll dive into the most widely-used editing software programs: Adobe Premiere Pro, Final Cut Pro, and DaVinci Resolve. We'll cover their primary functions, essential tools, and features that make them stand out. Whether you're a complete novice or familiar with some editing basics, this guide will provide practical instructions on starting a project, setting up a timeline, and importing footage. Additionally, we'll explore basic tools like cutting, trimming, and merging clips, and offer quick tips to improve efficiency as you work within the software.

Overview of Popular Video Editing Programs

There are many video editing programs available, each with its own strengths and special features. The choice of software depends on factors like budget, skill level, and the specific needs of your project. Below is an overview of the three most popular programs—Adobe Premiere Pro, Final Cut Pro, and DaVinci Resolve—along with some notable alternatives.

Adobe Premiere Pro

Adobe Premiere Pro is one of the most widely used video editing programs, known for its versatility and professional-grade features. Used by filmmakers, content creators, and even Hollywood studios, Premiere Pro offers a comprehensive set of tools for both simple edits and complex, multi-layered projects.

- **Strengths:**
  Premiere Pro is highly adaptable, with support for a variety of formats and resolutions. Its robust set of tools includes advanced color grading, multi-cam editing, and integration with Adobe's Creative Cloud suite, allowing for seamless workflows with Photoshop, After Effects, and more.

- **Best For:**

  Intermediate to advanced editors who want access to professional tools and features.

- **Subscription Model:**

  Adobe Premiere Pro is part of Adobe's Creative Cloud, which requires a monthly or annual subscription.

Final Cut Pro

Final Cut Pro is Apple's flagship video editing software, exclusive to Mac users. Known for its powerful features and intuitive design, Final Cut Pro is a favorite among professional editors who prefer the Mac ecosystem. Its performance is optimized for Apple hardware, which allows for fast rendering and smooth editing of high-resolution footage.

- **Strengths:**

  Final Cut Pro's "magnetic timeline" allows for easy rearrangement of clips without affecting the overall structure of the timeline. The software also provides excellent color grading tools, multi-cam editing, and advanced motion graphics.

- **Best For:**

  Intermediate to advanced editors who use Mac and want a one-time purchase software instead of a subscription.

- **Pricing:**

  Unlike Premiere Pro, Final Cut Pro is available as a one-time purchase, making it more cost-effective for long-term use.

DaVinci Resolve

DaVinci Resolve is widely known for its industry-leading color grading tools, which are used in Hollywood film production. It's a versatile editor with a free version that provides a significant range of features, making it popular with beginners and professionals alike.

- **Strengths:**

  DaVinci Resolve excels in color grading, offering precision tools that allow editors to adjust every aspect of a video's color. It also supports multi-track editing, 3D visual effects, and audio post-production, making it a powerful all-in-one program.

- **Best For:** All levels of editors, especially those who need advanced color grading and prefer a free or one-time purchase option.

- **Pricing:**
  DaVinci Resolve offers a free version with robust features, as well as a paid Studio version with additional advanced tools.

Other Notable Software Options

- **iMovie:** A free, beginner-friendly option available for Mac users, suitable for simple editing projects.

- **Filmora:** Known for its user-friendly interface and variety of effects, Filmora is popular with beginners and social media creators.

- **Avid Media Composer:** A professional-grade software used in Hollywood, known for its high-level editing features and audio controls.

Starting a Project: Setting Up Your Timeline and Importing Footage

Once you've chosen your editing software, the first step in any project is setting up your workspace, creating a new project, and importing your footage. Each editing software has a slightly different layout, but the steps to get started are generally similar.

1. Setting Up Your Project

- **Start a New Project:**

  Open your software and create a new project. You'll usually be prompted to name the project and select a save location. This is an excellent opportunity to organize your projects, so choose a descriptive name and a specific folder where all project files will be saved.

- **Adjust Project Settings:**

  Depending on your software, you may be asked to configure settings for your new project. Key settings include the resolution (e.g., 1080p, 4K) and frame rate (e.g., 24fps, 30fps). Choose settings that match the footage you're working with and the platform where the video will be published.

- **Create a Folder Structure:**

  A well-organized folder structure can save you time. Consider creating folders within your project file for raw footage, audio files, graphics, and exports. This structure will help keep everything in one place, making it easy to find specific files during editing.

2. Setting Up Your Timeline

The timeline is where you arrange your video clips, audio, and effects. It's the main workspace for editors, allowing you to visualize how your project will unfold.

- **Understanding Tracks:**

  Most timelines include multiple tracks for video, audio, and effects. Tracks are layered, meaning that the top layer will be visible over lower layers in the final video. Arrange clips in the appropriate tracks based on their role, such as placing dialogue on one track and background music on another.

- **Creating Sequence Settings:**

  In most software, sequences are where you organize each portion of your timeline. For example, in Adobe Premiere Pro, you'll set your sequence resolution, frame rate, and aspect ratio to match your project settings. In DaVinci Resolve, sequences are known as timelines.

- **Adding Markers and Labels:**

  Markers and labels can help organize your timeline, making it easier to keep track of important scenes or changes. Use markers to highlight specific points, such as where an effect should begin or where you want to add a transition.

3. Importing Footage

Importing footage is the process of bringing your video files, audio, and other assets into the software so that you can start editing.

- **Navigate to the Import Option:**

  Most programs have an "Import" or "Media Browser" function, allowing you to browse your computer for files. Adobe Premiere Pro, for instance, has a "Media Browser" panel that lets you drag files directly into the project panel.

- **Organize Footage in Bins or Folders:**

  Once your footage is imported, organize it into bins (folders within the software) based on categories like "interviews," "B-roll," or "graphics." This makes it easy to locate specific clips while editing.

- **Review and Select Clips:**

  Before you start editing, watch your footage and take note of key moments. This helps you identify the clips you want to use, saving you time in the editing process.

Basic Tools and Functions (Cut, Trim, Split, Merge, Timeline Navigation)

With your project set up and footage imported, it's time to explore the basic tools and functions that form the foundation of video editing. Here's an overview of essential tools you'll find in most editing software:

1. Cut Tool

- **Purpose:**
  The Cut tool, also known as the Razor or Slice tool in some programs, allows you to divide clips into smaller segments. This is especially useful for removing unwanted sections or isolating specific scenes.

- **How to Use It:**
  Select the Cut tool from your toolbar, then click on the clip in your timeline where you want to make a

division. The clip will split at that point, creating two separate segments.

2. Trim Tool

- **Purpose:**
  Trimming lets you shorten or extend a clip's duration by adjusting its starting or ending points. Trimming is useful for refining cuts and ensuring smooth transitions.

- **How to Use It:**
  Hover over the edge of a clip on the timeline until you see the trim cursor (usually a bracket icon). Drag the edge inward to shorten or outward to lengthen the clip.

3. Split Tool

- **Purpose:**
  Splitting a clip separates it into different parts, allowing you to rearrange scenes or add transitions between them. This is especially useful when editing longer clips or rearranging sequences.

- **How to Use It:**

In most software, you can use the same tool as the Cut or Razor tool. Select the point where you want to divide the clip, then click to split it into sections.

4. Merge or Group

- **Purpose:**
  Merging or grouping clips allows you to treat multiple clips as one unit, making it easier to move and apply effects to several clips simultaneously.

- **How to Use It:**

  Select the clips you want to merge, right-click, and choose "Group" or "Merge" (depending on your software). This groups the clips into one unit, which you can ungroup if needed.

5. Timeline Navigation

- **Purpose:**
  Navigation tools make it easier to move through your project, zoom in for detailed work, and manage playback. Proper timeline navigation helps you work more efficiently and focus on specific segments.

- **Key Navigation Tools:**

Playhead: The playhead is a vertical line that shows where you are on the timeline. Move it to review specific parts of your video.

Zoom: Most software has zoom controls, allowing you to zoom in on the timeline for precision or zoom out for a broader view.

Scrubbing: Scrubbing involves dragging the playhead across the timeline to quickly preview your footage.

Quick Tips for Improving Efficiency Within the Software

Efficient editing saves time and makes the process smoother. Here are some quick tips for improving efficiency within your editing software:

1. **Learn Keyboard Shortcuts:**

   Each software has a set of keyboard shortcuts that allow you to perform actions quickly. For example, pressing "C" in Premiere Pro activates the Cut tool, while "V" switches to the Selection tool.

2. **Use Proxy Files for Large Projects:**

   Editing high-resolution footage can slow down your system. Creating proxy files (lower-resolution versions of your clips) can help speed up your workflow, especially with 4K or higher files.

3. **Take Advantage of Presets:**

   Many programs come with effect, color, and transition presets. Use these to save time when applying standard settings, then customize as needed.

4. **Use Auto-Save or Backup Options:**

   Editing software can be demanding on your computer, which can lead to crashes. Enable auto-save to prevent data loss and consider backing up your project files periodically.

5. **Create Templates for Repeated Projects:**

   If you frequently create similar types of videos, set up templates with pre-arranged timelines, text styles, and common effects. This allows you to save time on setup and focus on content.

By understanding the basics of popular video editing software and familiarizing yourself with essential tools and functions, you're setting the foundation for effective and creative editing. Starting a project, organizing your timeline, and mastering basic tools allow you to work confidently, setting you up for success in more advanced techniques as you progress. Video editing software is an extensive toolkit, and by exploring these features, you'll gain the skills needed to turn raw footage into a compelling story.

CHAPTER 3

Building a Strong Foundation with Core Editing Skills

A polished video edit is more than just a collection of scenes put together; it's a carefully crafted experience that guides viewers through a story, captures attention, and delivers a message. Mastering core editing skills is crucial for creating videos that look professional, flow seamlessly, and engage audiences. These foundational techniques form the building blocks of effective video editing, allowing you to refine raw footage and shape it into a cohesive narrative.

In this chapter, we'll focus on essential skills every video editor should master. From cutting and trimming footage to applying transitions, understanding timing and pacing, and using B-roll to enhance storytelling, each technique we'll explore serves a specific purpose in creating smooth, engaging videos. By the end of this chapter, you'll have the tools and knowledge to create videos with confidence, using these techniques to produce content that captivates and resonates with your audience.

Cutting and Trimming Footage for Smooth Transitions

Cutting and trimming footage is one of the most basic, yet most powerful, editing skills. Cutting refers to the act of splitting a clip into separate sections, while trimming involves adjusting the beginning or end of a clip to shorten or lengthen it. Together, cutting and trimming help control the pacing, eliminate unnecessary footage, and ensure smooth transitions between scenes.

Cutting: Creating Seamless Connections Between Shots

- **Purpose of Cutting:**

  Cutting allows you to divide footage, isolate specific moments, and control what the viewer sees. By cutting at the right moments, you can guide the viewer's attention, emphasize important actions or emotions, and maintain continuity. For instance, cutting from a wide shot to a close-up draws the viewer's focus to a particular detail or reaction.

- **Types of Cuts:**

  There are several types of cuts commonly used in video editing, each with a specific effect on pacing and mood:

- o **Straight Cut:** A simple transition from one shot to another, commonly used in dialogues or to connect two different scenes.

- o **Jump Cut:** A cut within the same scene that shows a change in time, often used to speed up a sequence (e.g., showing someone packing a suitcase in several quick cuts).

- o **Cutaway:** A cut to a different shot that provides context or additional information, such as showing a clock to indicate the passing of time.

- **Techniques for Effective Cutting:**

When cutting, aim to cut on the action to create smooth, natural transitions. For example, if someone is reaching to open a door, cut from the wide shot to a close-up as their hand touches the doorknob. This technique, known as "cutting on the action," creates a sense of fluidity and continuity, reducing the chance of a jarring jump.

Trimming: Refining the Start and End of Each Shot

- **Purpose of Trimming:**

  Trimming helps you adjust the length of each clip, removing unwanted parts at the beginning or end to keep scenes focused and concise. For instance, trimming a few seconds of dead air before someone starts speaking can create a cleaner, more professional look.

- **Using In and Out Points:**

  Most editing software allows you to set "in" and "out" points, which define where a clip starts and ends. This lets you select specific moments within a longer clip and save time during the editing process.

- **Practical Tips for Trimming:**

  Trim with purpose, focusing on the essential moments. Avoid lingering too long on any shot unless it serves a deliberate purpose, like building suspense. Consistent trimming keeps the pacing tight, prevents viewer fatigue, and ensures that every second on screen contributes to the story.

Adding and Adjusting Transitions (Fade, Cross-Dissolve, etc.)

Transitions are visual effects that help guide viewers from one scene to the next. While simple cuts work well in most cases, transitions like fades and dissolves can add depth, emotion, or pacing to a video. Effective use of transitions can enhance the flow of your video and emphasize shifts in tone or time.

Types of Transitions and Their Uses

1. **Fade In/Fade Out:**

   A fade in starts with a blank screen that gradually reveals the footage, while a fade out gradually darkens the footage until the screen is blank. Fades are commonly used at the beginning or end of a video or scene, creating a soft opening or closing.

2. **Cross-Dissolve:**

   A cross-dissolve blends two scenes, causing the first to fade out as the second fades in. This transition is useful for scenes with a continuous flow or similar mood, as it provides a gentle, subtle shift.

3. **Wipe:**

   Wipes move a line or shape across the screen to

replace one scene with another. Wipes are a stylistic choice often used in genres that embrace unique transitions, such as action sequences or humorous videos.

4. **Zoom or Spin Transitions:**

These dynamic transitions add a fast-paced or stylized effect, often used in music videos or trailers. However, use them sparingly, as excessive or complex transitions can distract from the content.

When to Use Transitions

The key to using transitions effectively is restraint. Overusing transitions can make a video feel cluttered and amateurish. Use them to:

- Indicate a shift in time or location, such as a fade out to transition between scenes set at different times.

- Emphasize emotional shifts, using cross-dissolves or fades to soften the transition.

- Create pacing effects, such as using quick cuts or dynamic transitions to speed up an action scene.

Adjusting Transition Duration and Timing

The duration of a transition affects its impact on the viewer. Shorter transitions are fast and subtle, ideal for scenes where you want a quick change, while longer transitions are better suited for moments of reflection or mood shifts.

Most editing software allows you to adjust transition duration by dragging the edges of the transition effect on the timeline. Experiment with different durations to find the timing that best suits your video's flow.

Understanding and Applying Timing and Pacing in Edits

Timing and pacing are central to creating an engaging video. They control the rhythm of the story, affecting how viewers perceive each scene and emotion. Proper timing can enhance suspense, excitement, or drama, while poor pacing can lead to viewer disengagement.

Timing: Knowing When to Cut

Timing refers to the precise moment you cut from one shot to the next. Good timing depends on the natural rhythm of the scene and the action within it. For example:

- **Cutting on the Action:** Cut at the moment of action, like a character reaching for an object or turning their head. This makes transitions feel smooth and natural.

- **Anticipating Viewer Expectations:** Timing can manipulate viewer expectations. For example, if an audience expects a cut after a character's dialogue, you can create suspense by delaying the cut for a moment.

Pacing: Controlling the Speed of the Story

Pacing controls the overall speed of a video. Faster pacing builds excitement, while slower pacing allows for reflection. Here are some practical tips for pacing:

- **Match Pacing to Content:** A quick pace works well for action scenes or montages, while a slower pace suits dramatic or emotional moments.

- **Alternate Between Fast and Slow Pacing:** Alternating between quick and slow scenes can add variety, keeping the audience engaged. For instance, after a high-energy scene, use a slower-paced scene to allow viewers a moment to process the events.

Using Music and Sound for Timing and Pacing

Music is an effective tool for guiding timing and pacing. For example, you can cut to the beat of a song for rhythmic editing or slow the pace of cuts during softer music to create a contemplative feel. Adjusting your edits to match audio cues reinforces the mood and structure of the video.

Using B-Roll Effectively to Enhance Storytelling

B-roll refers to supplementary footage that provides context, enhances storytelling, or fills in gaps in the primary footage (known as A-roll). For example, in a travel video, A-roll might be a narrator discussing a location, while B-roll includes shots of landmarks, street scenes, and cultural events.

Purposes of B-Roll

1. **Adding Visual Interest:**

   B-roll prevents the video from becoming monotonous by adding variety. In a documentary, for instance, B-roll could include shots of the setting or related activities, enhancing the viewer's understanding and interest.

2. **Providing Context and Detail:**

    B-roll offers context that helps explain the main
    footage. In an interview, cutaways to relevant B-roll
    (such as the subject working or interacting with their
    environment) provide viewers with a visual
    narrative.

3. **Covering Edits and Transitions:**

    B-roll can hide cuts or cover awkward transitions.
    For example, if you need to cut part of a speaker's
    dialogue, you can use B-roll to cover the edit,
    creating a seamless transition between shots.

Choosing Effective B-Roll

Selecting the right B-roll is crucial. Good B-roll adds to the
story rather than distracting from it. Here are some
guidelines for choosing effective B-roll:

- **Match the Theme or Subject Matter:** Choose
  footage that enhances the main content. If the A-roll
  discusses a community event, B-roll should show
  people participating, decorations, and other relevant
  visuals.

- **Capture Different Angles and Perspectives:** Use a mix of wide, medium, and close-up shots to add visual variety and depth. For instance, a travel video might show a wide shot of a city skyline, a medium shot of a bustling market, and a close-up of a vendor preparing food.

Integrating B-Roll with A-Roll

Integrating B-roll requires balancing it with the A-roll. Here are some techniques:

- **Cutaways:** Use cutaways to switch from A-roll to B-roll, providing a natural way to show additional context or details. This technique is especially effective in interviews, where B-roll helps break up talking-head shots.

- **Layering B-Roll Over Audio:** Layering B-roll over audio from the A-roll, such as narration or dialogue, helps maintain continuity while adding visual interest. For instance, in a documentary, layering B-roll over the narrator's voice can reinforce key points.

Building a strong foundation with core editing skills is essential for any aspiring video editor. From cutting and trimming footage to applying thoughtful transitions, mastering timing and pacing, and using B-roll effectively, these skills form the backbone of professional, engaging video content. Each technique serves a purpose in enhancing the storytelling, guiding the viewer's attention, and maintaining a natural flow.

As you continue practicing and applying these techniques, you'll develop a keen eye for what works best in different contexts. The more you work on these foundational skills, the more confident you'll become in crafting videos that not only look polished but also resonate with viewers.

CHAPTER 4

Enhancing Visual Appeal with Color Correction and Grading

Color is a powerful tool in video production. It shapes mood, draws attention, and enhances storytelling. While it might seem subtle to some viewers, color correction and color grading are essential components of video editing that can transform raw footage into visually stunning content. These techniques are crucial for achieving a professional look, ensuring consistent visuals, and creating a particular atmosphere in your videos.

Color correction and grading may seem like advanced skills, but they're achievable with practice and understanding of some basic principles. This chapter will guide you through the essentials, helping you understand the role of color correction and grading, the difference between the two, and how to apply them effectively to improve the visual quality and mood of your videos.

In this chapter, we'll cover the basics of color correction, where you'll learn how to adjust brightness, contrast, and white balance. We'll then delve into color grading to set the mood and introduce Look-Up Tables (LUTs) to maintain a consistent style. Finally, we'll explore tips for achieving a cinematic look that enhances the storytelling and immerses your viewers.

Color Correction Fundamentals: Adjusting Brightness, Contrast, and White Balance

Before diving into color grading, it's essential to master color correction, which ensures that your footage has a clean, accurate look. Color correction is the process of adjusting the colors, brightness, and contrast in your footage to make it look as true to life as possible. Think of it as fixing imperfections in the raw footage—getting it to a neutral base before applying stylized color effects.

1. Adjusting Brightness and Exposure

Brightness, or exposure, is the amount of light in your video footage. Sometimes, footage may be overexposed (too bright) or underexposed (too dark) due to varying lighting conditions during filming. Correcting brightness is crucial for making the video visually appealing and ensuring that details are visible.

- **Increasing Brightness for Underexposed Footage:** When footage appears too dark, adjust the brightness or exposure slider in your editing software. Start by increasing exposure incrementally until you can see details clearly, but be cautious not to make it look unnatural.

- **Lowering Brightness for Overexposed Footage:** Overexposed footage may have overly bright areas, causing details to be lost. Lowering the exposure can bring back some of these details, but there are limits, as overexposure can permanently wash out certain parts of the image. Try reducing highlights specifically if your software allows, as this often restores details in bright areas.

2. Adjusting Contrast

Contrast is the difference between the darkest and lightest parts of an image. Increasing contrast can make images look sharper and more dynamic, while lowering contrast creates a softer look. Correct contrast levels give depth to the image, making it visually striking.

- **Increasing Contrast for Depth and Definition:** For footage that appears flat or washed out, increasing contrast can create depth and make subjects stand out. Be mindful, however, as too much contrast can cause dark areas to lose detail.

- **Balancing Shadows and Highlights:** In most video editing software, you can adjust shadows and highlights separately, allowing you to create contrast while preserving details. Increasing the shadows can darken the darkest parts, while decreasing highlights can soften the lightest areas.

3. Adjusting White Balance

White balance is crucial for achieving accurate colors. Different lighting conditions (natural daylight, fluorescent light, tungsten) cast different color temperatures, and adjusting white balance corrects these shifts. Improper white balance can make footage look too blue, yellow, or green, so getting this adjustment right is essential.

- **Understanding Color Temperature:** Color temperature ranges from cool (blue) to warm (yellow/red). Daylight has a higher color temperature, making it appear cooler, while indoor lighting often has a lower temperature, adding a warmer tone. Adjusting white balance neutralizes these tones, ensuring that whites look true to life.

- **Using the Eyedropper Tool:**

   Many editing programs provide an eyedropper tool for setting white balance. Simply select the eyedropper and click on a part of the video that should be pure white or neutral gray. The software will adjust the entire image based on this reference, balancing the colors to achieve a neutral look.

- **Manual White Balance Controls:**

   If your software doesn't have an eyedropper, you can manually adjust the color temperature and tint sliders. Move the temperature slider to the right to add warmth (yellow) or to the left to cool down the image (blue). Adjust the tint slider to remove any green or magenta tint that may be present.

By focusing on brightness, contrast, and white balance, color correction makes your footage look natural and consistent, setting the foundation for color grading, which will add artistic style and mood.

Introduction to Color Grading and Setting the Mood

Color grading takes corrected footage and enhances it to create a specific look, mood, or style. Grading allows you to add a cinematic feel, emphasize emotions, and build atmosphere, whether you're aiming for a warm, nostalgic tone or a cool, suspenseful effect.

1. Understanding the Purpose of Color Grading

Color grading is used to establish the emotional undertone of a video. For example:

- **Warm, Saturated Tones:** Often used for happy, lively scenes, with emphasis on colors like yellow, orange, and red.

- **Cool, Desaturated Tones:** Often used for somber or mysterious scenes, focusing on colors like blue and green, with lower saturation levels.

- **High-Contrast Looks:** Creates a dramatic feel, often used in action or thriller genres, where the difference between light and dark colors is more pronounced.

2. Basic Tools for Color Grading

Most editing software provides basic tools for color grading, including color wheels, curves, and saturation controls. Here's how each of these tools can help shape the mood of your video:

- **Color Wheels:** Color wheels allow you to adjust colors in different parts of the tonal range—shadows, midtones, and highlights. Adjusting the shadows, for example, adds color to darker areas, while adjusting highlights affects the brightest areas.

- **Curves:** Curves allow precise control over brightness and color in specific parts of the image. By manipulating the curve, you can create customized adjustments, such as boosting contrast only in midtones or adding color to shadows.

- **Saturation:** Saturation controls the intensity of colors in your footage. Increasing saturation makes colors more vivid, while decreasing it results in a muted, grayscale effect. Adjusting saturation selectively (for example, boosting blues but lowering greens) creates unique, stylized looks.

3. Creating Mood with Color Grading

To set a specific mood, think about how different colors affect emotions and perception. Here are some examples:

- **Warm Tones for Happiness and Comfort:** Warm colors, such as orange, yellow, and red, evoke feelings of happiness, nostalgia, and warmth. This is often achieved by increasing warmth in the highlights and slightly boosting reds in midtones.

- **Cool Tones for Calmness or Suspense:** Cool colors like blue and green create feelings of calmness, distance, or suspense. This can be achieved by adding blue to the shadows and reducing warmth in the highlights.

- **Desaturated Colors for Seriousness:** Lowering the saturation while keeping contrast high can give footage a raw, serious tone. This is common in dramas or historical films to create a gritty, realistic feel.

Color grading is an artistic process that allows for creativity. Experiment with different adjustments to see how they affect the mood, and find a style that complements the story you want to tell.

Using LUTs (Look-Up Tables) for Style and Consistency

Look-Up Tables, or LUTs, are pre-set color adjustments that apply a consistent look to your footage. LUTs are widely used in the industry to create cohesive styles quickly, as they contain predefined color transformations that are applied to raw footage.

1. What Are LUTs?

LUTs are essentially color profiles that map one set of colors to another, changing the way colors look across an entire clip. They allow you to apply a specific style, such as "film look" or "vintage," without needing to manually adjust individual color settings. LUTs are especially useful for ensuring that footage shot at different times or in different lighting conditions looks cohesive.

2. Types of LUTs

There are two primary types of LUTs:

- **Technical LUTs:** Used to standardize footage, such as converting a log profile to a Rec. 709 color space. Technical LUTs help maintain accurate color balance and contrast.

- **Creative LUTs:** Designed for stylistic effects, creative LUTs add unique color grading profiles, giving footage a distinct look (e.g., sepia tones, teal-orange). These LUTs can dramatically change the tone and mood of your footage with minimal effort.

3. Applying LUTs in Editing Software

Most editing software includes a way to apply LUTs to your footage. Look for an "Effects" or "Color" tab in your software, where you'll find an option to import or apply LUTs. Once you apply a LUT, you can usually adjust its intensity, fine-tune individual color settings, or stack multiple LUTs for a customized look.

4. Customizing LUTs

While LUTs provide a quick way to add style, they may not perfectly match your footage. Consider LUTs as a starting point, then make further adjustments to fine-tune the colors. For example, if a LUT makes skin tones too saturated, lower the saturation or adjust specific color channels to correct it.

LUTs save time and ensure style consistency, but remember that every video is unique. Customize your LUTs to complement the content and story.

Tips for Achieving a Cinematic Look

Achieving a cinematic look involves a combination of color correction, grading, and a few stylistic choices. Here are some tips for making your footage look cinematic:

1. Use Subtle Color Grading

Cinematic color grading is often subtle, focusing on balanced colors with slight emphasis on certain tones, like teal and orange. Teal tones in shadows and orange in highlights can create contrast that enhances skin tones and adds depth, making the footage look professional.

2. Control Depth with Contrast and Exposure

Cinematic footage often has a controlled contrast level. Avoid overly bright or dark areas that obscure detail. Gradual changes in contrast across the image can add depth and make the scene look well-lit and visually pleasing.

3. Emphasize Natural Skin Tones

One key to a cinematic look is natural-looking skin tones. Make sure your color grading doesn't distort skin tones, as this is noticeable and can make footage look unrealistic. Adjust color wheels and midtones if skin appears too red, yellow, or green.

4. Use Vignetting Sparingly

Adding a subtle vignette (a darkening around the edges of the frame) can guide the viewer's attention toward the center, enhancing focus and adding a cinematic feel. Keep vignetting subtle to avoid distraction.

5. Adjust for the Right Saturation

A cinematic look often involves muted colors, but with select colors (like greens or blues) slightly emphasized. Experiment with lowering saturation for most colors, then selectively enhancing specific tones for a balanced, eye-catching result.

Color correction and grading are powerful tools that enhance the visual appeal of your videos, helping you create a professional and cinematic look. Color correction establishes a neutral base by adjusting brightness, contrast, and white balance, while color grading adds mood and emotion through stylized color adjustments. With the use of LUTs for consistency and practical tips for cinematic quality, you're now equipped to take your video editing to the next level. Mastering these techniques will not only improve your videos' quality but also deepen the emotional impact they have on viewers.

CHAPTER 5

Working with Sound: Music, Voiceovers, and Sound Effects

Audio is a vital component of video editing, as it significantly enhances the viewer's experience, mood, and engagement. While visuals capture attention, audio maintains it, creating an immersive environment that supports storytelling. High-quality audio is not just about music or voiceover clarity; it's about creating a well-balanced soundscape that complements the visuals and delivers the intended emotional impact.

Many beginner editors overlook the importance of sound, focusing primarily on visual elements. However, in professional editing, sound and visuals work hand-in-hand to tell the story. Poor audio quality or a lack of audio balance can distract viewers and diminish the overall impact of the video. This chapter will guide you through the essentials of working with sound, from balancing background music, dialogue, and sound effects to syncing audio with visuals, using sound effects effectively, and cleaning up audio with noise reduction tools.

The Importance of Audio: Creating the Right Soundscape

Soundscape refers to the overall audio environment within a video, including dialogue, music, sound effects, and background ambiance. An effective soundscape supports the visuals, enhances storytelling, and sets the tone for each scene. Let's explore the core elements that contribute to a well-designed soundscape:

1. Setting the Mood with Background Music

Music is one of the most impactful audio elements in a video, as it sets the tone and evokes emotions. Whether it's a cheerful, upbeat tune in a travel vlog or a suspenseful score in a thriller, background music creates an emotional layer that complements the visuals.

- **Matching Music to the Scene:** Choose music that aligns with the mood of the scene. For example, use a slow, calm melody for reflective moments or fast-paced music for action scenes.

- **Avoiding Overpowering Music:** While background music is essential, it should not overpower dialogue or sound effects. Adjust the volume so that it complements, rather than dominates, other audio elements.

2. Dialogue: Ensuring Clarity and Presence

Dialogue is a primary form of storytelling in many videos, providing context, information, or narrative. Clear and intelligible dialogue is crucial for viewer comprehension and engagement.

- **Prioritizing Dialogue:** Ensure dialogue is the most prominent audio layer, particularly when used for storytelling or explanations. Background music and sound effects should be secondary to dialogue.

- **Adjusting Volume and EQ for Clarity:** Boost frequencies around 1,000-4,000 Hz to enhance voice clarity. Avoid heavy bass or treble that could distort spoken words.

3. Sound Effects: Adding Depth and Realism

Sound effects create a sense of realism and emphasize actions in the video, such as footsteps, door creaks, or ambient sounds like birds chirping.

- **Purposeful Sound Effects:** Use sound effects to highlight specific actions or transitions, like the swoosh of a moving object or a camera shutter sound in a photography sequence.

- **Layering Effects for Depth:** Combine multiple sound effects, like footsteps with ambient street noise, to add a richer audio texture to your video.

A well-crafted soundscape is subtle yet powerful, enhancing the visuals without drawing undue attention to the audio itself. Striking the right balance in your soundscape ensures an immersive experience that holds the viewer's attention.

Balancing Background Music, Dialogue, and Sound Effects

Achieving a balanced audio mix is essential for a professional, polished video. A balanced mix ensures that no single audio element overpowers another, creating a harmonious blend that is easy for viewers to follow. Here's how to balance background music, dialogue, and sound effects effectively:

1. Using Volume Levels for Balance

Each audio element should have a specific volume level, ensuring it is audible but not overwhelming. Follow these general guidelines:

- **Dialogue:** Keep dialogue at the forefront, with a volume level that makes speech clear and intelligible. A typical range for dialogue is -12 dB to -6 dB, depending on the loudness of the voice and background sounds.

- **Background Music:** Lower background music to avoid overpowering dialogue. A good rule of thumb is to keep it around -20 dB to -15 dB when paired with dialogue.

- **Sound Effects:** Sound effects should be louder than background music but quieter than dialogue, typically around -15 dB to -10 dB. Adjust each effect based on its importance in the scene.

2. Using Audio Ducking for Clarity

Audio ducking automatically lowers the volume of background music when dialogue or a prominent sound effect is present. This technique ensures that dialogue remains the main focus without removing the music entirely.

- **Applying Ducking in Editing Software:** Most video editing software offers an audio ducking feature. Select the dialogue track as the primary audio, and apply ducking to the background music track. This will reduce music volume when dialogue occurs, and it will gradually return to normal when the dialogue ends.

3. Equalizing Audio Frequencies

Equalization (EQ) adjusts specific frequencies within an audio track to ensure clarity and prevent clashing sounds. Different audio elements occupy different frequency ranges, and EQ allows you to fine-tune these ranges to avoid overcrowding.

- **Dialogue Frequencies:** Boost frequencies between 1,000-4,000 Hz for voice clarity and reduce unnecessary bass.

- **Music Frequencies:** Lower the midrange frequencies in background music (around 1,000-4,000 Hz) to avoid interfering with dialogue.

- **Sound Effects Frequencies:** Adjust sound effects based on their characteristics. High-pitched effects may benefit from boosting higher frequencies, while ambient sounds may require more bass for a fuller presence.

By balancing volume levels, applying audio ducking, and using EQ, you can create a well-mixed audio track where dialogue, music, and sound effects complement each other.

Syncing Audio with Visuals and Cutting on Beat

Synchronization is essential to make audio feel connected to the visuals. Properly syncing audio with visuals strengthens the impact of actions, emotions, and transitions in the video. Here's how to sync audio effectively:

1. Syncing Dialogue and Voiceovers

For videos with recorded dialogue or voiceovers, syncing the audio with the visuals ensures that the viewer remains engaged and understands the narrative.

- **Matching Lip Movements:** Ensure that spoken words align with lip movements, especially in videos with dialogue. Misaligned audio is distracting and can undermine the quality of the video.

- **Adjusting Timing for Emphasis:** Use slight timing adjustments to emphasize important words or phrases by syncing them with specific actions, like the character pointing or the camera zooming in.

2. Cutting on Beat for Musical Rhythm

In videos with music, cutting on the beat is an editing technique that creates a natural rhythm by aligning cuts with the music's tempo. This technique is widely used in music videos, trailers, and montages.

- **Finding the Beat:** Listen to the music track and identify the beats, often using markers in your editing software. Each beat is an opportunity to cut or transition between scenes, enhancing the flow.

- **Creating a Rhythm with Visuals:** Cutting on the beat is especially effective in fast-paced scenes or highlight reels. For slower scenes, consider cutting on every second or third beat to maintain a more relaxed pace.

3. Synchronizing Sound Effects with Actions

Sound effects should align precisely with on-screen actions, enhancing the realism and immersion of the video. For example, if a character slams a door, the door slam sound effect should match the visual exactly.

- **Using Frame-by-Frame Adjustments:** Most editing software allows frame-by-frame adjustments.

Use these to align sound effects precisely with actions, ensuring accuracy in timing.

- **Layering Effects for Impact:** Combine multiple sound effects to emphasize impactful moments. For example, layering the sound of an explosion with subtle glass-breaking and debris-falling sounds adds realism and depth.

Syncing audio with visuals is crucial for maintaining the viewer's attention and reinforcing the connection between what they see and hear.

Using Sound Effects Purposefully to Enhance the Story

Sound effects are valuable storytelling tools that emphasize actions, add realism, and help convey emotions. However, using sound effects purposefully—rather than excessively—ensures they enhance rather than distract from the narrative.

1. Emphasizing Key Actions with Sound Effects

Sound effects can bring attention to important actions, such as footsteps, door creaks, or car engines. Using sound effects for these moments enhances immersion, making viewers feel like they're part of the scene.

- **Choosing Sounds Carefully:** Select sounds that match the environment and tone of the scene. For example, use softer footsteps on carpet and louder, echoing steps on hard floors.

- **Adjusting Volume for Realism:** Balance sound effects volume with the surrounding audio. For distant actions, use a lower volume, and for close-up actions, increase the volume for prominence.

2. Adding Depth and Texture to Scenes

Ambient sound effects, such as birds chirping, wind rustling, or city noise, add layers to your audio track, creating a realistic background. This additional texture immerses viewers in the environment, whether it's a bustling city or a peaceful forest.

- **Layering Ambience for Richness:** Combine multiple ambient sounds to create a fuller, more immersive soundscape. For example, a city scene could include traffic, voices, and faint music in the background.

- **Using Background Effects Subtly:** Keep ambient sounds subtle so that they enhance rather than distract. The goal is to create a natural atmosphere that complements, not overshadows, the main audio elements.

3. Conveying Emotions with Sound Effects

Certain sound effects, such as ominous tones, heartbeat sounds, or whispers, can add emotional depth. These effects are commonly used in genres like horror or drama to create tension, suspense, or intimacy.

- **Building Tension with Subtle Effects:** Add faint, unsettling sounds in suspenseful scenes to create unease. Avoid making the effect too loud, as subtlety enhances suspense without giving away the impact.

- **Expressing Excitement with Impactful Sounds:** For action scenes, use louder, sharper sound effects, such as gunshots or crashes, to emphasize excitement and intensity.

Using sound effects purposefully, rather than excessively, supports storytelling and keeps viewers engaged.

Cleaning Up Audio with Noise Reduction Tools

Background noise, such as static, hum, or wind, can detract from audio clarity. Noise reduction tools help remove unwanted sounds, enhancing audio quality and making dialogue or music more distinct.

1. Identifying and Isolating Noise

Before applying noise reduction, listen to your audio to identify any unwanted background sounds. Use headphones for better detection, as subtle noises may not be noticeable through speakers.

- **Common Noises to Reduce:** Look for consistent hums, buzzes, wind noise, or static that doesn't contribute to the scene.

2. Applying Noise Reduction in Editing Software

Most video editing software includes noise reduction tools, often found in the audio effects or filters section. These tools reduce unwanted sounds without affecting the main audio.

- **Using Noise Reduction Presets:** Start with the software's built-in presets, which often provide effective reduction for common noises. Adjust the settings based on your specific noise issues.

- **Manual Reduction with Noise Profile:** In advanced programs, you can select a sample of background noise to create a "noise profile." The software then applies noise reduction to similar sounds throughout the track.

3. Avoiding Overuse of Noise Reduction

Excessive noise reduction can distort audio, making dialogue sound muffled or robotic. Strike a balance between reducing noise and preserving the natural sound of your audio.

- **Applying Gradual Reduction:** Instead of reducing noise drastically, apply gradual reduction to maintain clarity and avoid artifacts.

- **Layering Noise Reduction with EQ:** Use EQ to cut unwanted frequencies and complement noise reduction. For example, reduce low frequencies to remove hum while maintaining high frequencies for clarity.

Cleaning up audio ensures that viewers can focus on dialogue and key sounds without being distracted by unwanted noise.

Working with sound is a critical aspect of video editing that greatly influences the quality and engagement of your final product. By understanding the role of audio, balancing music, dialogue, and sound effects, syncing audio with visuals, using sound effects purposefully, and applying noise reduction, you can create a soundscape that enhances storytelling and keeps viewers immersed.

High-quality audio makes a video feel professional, drawing viewers into the story and supporting the visuals seamlessly. By mastering these techniques, you'll be equipped to produce videos with clear, balanced, and compelling audio that leaves a lasting impression on your audience.

CHAPTER 6

Adding Text, Titles, and Graphics

Text and graphics play an essential role in video production, helping to convey information, highlight key points, and engage viewers more effectively. When used correctly, text, titles, and graphics complement the visual narrative, adding clarity, depth, and professional polish to the content. However, when overused or poorly executed, these elements can clutter the screen and distract from the core message of the video.

Incorporating text and graphics into a video requires a careful balance. From choosing the right fonts and colors to placing titles and using animations, each choice influences the viewer's experience. This chapter explores the fundamentals of adding titles, lower thirds, and credits, selecting readable fonts, using animations effectively, and integrating motion graphics to enhance storytelling. By mastering these techniques, you'll be able to create videos that are visually engaging and informative, without compromising on readability or style.

Adding Titles, Lower Thirds, and Credits

Titles, lower thirds, and credits are key elements in video editing, each serving a distinct purpose. When applied thoughtfully, they enhance professionalism and structure, guiding the viewer's attention and providing context.

1. Titles

Titles introduce viewers to the main content or sections within a video. They are typically placed at the beginning of the video or used as section headers throughout the content.

- **Opening Titles:**

  Opening titles provide an immediate understanding of the video's theme, drawing viewers in. They usually include the video's title, subtitle, and sometimes the creator's name. Make sure opening titles are clear and attention-grabbing, setting the tone for the rest of the video.

- **Chapter or Section Titles:**

  In longer videos, especially tutorials or educational content, section titles help break down the content into digestible segments. These titles serve as visual markers, guiding viewers through the video and giving them context about each section.

2. Lower Thirds

Lower thirds are graphic overlays that appear in the lower portion of the screen. They're commonly used to introduce speakers, provide additional context, or offer brief information without interrupting the main content.

- **Speaker Identification:**

  In interviews, documentaries, or news-style videos, lower thirds introduce speakers by name, job title, or affiliation. This brief introduction gives viewers essential context about who's speaking.

- **Additional Information:**

  Lower thirds are also useful for displaying brief, supplementary information, such as the name of a location, dates, or event details. Use them sparingly to avoid overwhelming viewers with text.

3. Credits

Credits are usually placed at the end of a video, acknowledging contributors such as crew members, actors, or sponsors. They serve to recognize the work that went into the production and provide any necessary attributions.

- **End Credits:**

    End credits are a common way to conclude a video, listing names and roles of everyone involved. Keep end credits simple and concise, especially if the list is long, by limiting each line to essential information.

- **Attribution and Licensing Information:**

    If your video includes music, images, or other elements that require attribution, include this information in the credits. This ensures you respect copyright laws and comply with licensing agreements.

Choosing Fonts and Styles for Readability and Impact

Choosing the right fonts and styles for titles and graphics is crucial for readability and aesthetic appeal. The wrong font can be distracting or hard to read, detracting from the video's message. Consider these best practices for selecting fonts and styles that enhance your content.

1. Choosing the Right Font

Font choice significantly affects readability, style, and tone. Here's how to choose fonts that align with the video's purpose:

- **Serif vs. Sans Serif Fonts:**

  Serif fonts (like Times New Roman) have small decorative lines, which make them look formal and traditional. Sans-serif fonts (like Arial) lack these lines, giving a clean, modern look. For digital media, sans-serif fonts are generally more legible, especially on smaller screens.

- **Using Clean and Simple Fonts:**

  Avoid overly decorative or complex fonts, as they can be difficult to read. Fonts like Helvetica, Arial, and Roboto are popular choices for their clarity and simplicity, suitable for titles and lower thirds.

- **Establishing a Hierarchy with Different Fonts:** Using different fonts for titles, subtitles, and body text creates a visual hierarchy. For example, a bold font for the main title and a lighter font for subtitles or lower thirds helps guide viewers' eyes naturally across the screen.

2. Font Size and Spacing

Font size and spacing are equally important for readability, especially on smaller screens like mobile devices.

- **Font Size Guidelines:**

  Titles should be large enough to grab attention but not so large that they dominate the screen. For lower thirds, a font size that is legible but unobtrusive works best. Test font sizes across various screen sizes to ensure readability.

- **Line Spacing and Letter Spacing:**

  Proper spacing between lines and letters improves readability. Avoid crowding text by adjusting the spacing if needed, making sure each line of text is easily distinguishable.

3. Selecting Font Colors and Contrast

Choosing the right color for text ensures it stands out against the video background without being too jarring.

- **Using High Contrast for Visibility:**

  Text should contrast with the background color for maximum visibility. If your video has a bright background, opt for dark text, and vice versa. Black and white are common choices, but experiment with other colors that align with your video's color scheme.

- **Using Shadows and Outlines for Emphasis:** Shadows and outlines can make text stand out on complex backgrounds. A subtle shadow or thin outline can enhance readability without cluttering the screen.

Using Animations and Transitions for Text and Graphics

Animations and transitions can add dynamism to text and graphics, making them more engaging. However, overusing animations can lead to distraction. Here are some effective ways to apply animations and transitions.

1. Subtle Entry and Exit Animations

Adding entry and exit animations, like fades, slides, or pop-ups, gives text a smooth appearance and keeps viewers engaged. Subtlety is key, as excessive or flashy animations can take attention away from the video content.

- **Fade In and Fade Out:**

  Fades are a simple yet elegant choice for text entry and exit, allowing text to appear and disappear without abrupt transitions. Use this effect for lower thirds and titles for a professional look.

- **Slide Transitions:**

  Slide transitions allow text to enter or exit the screen from any direction. This effect is particularly useful for lower thirds, as it brings attention to the information without being intrusive.

2. Applying Consistent Animation Styles

Using consistent animations across text and graphics helps create a cohesive look. For example, if you use slide-ins for titles, apply similar motion to lower thirds and other on-screen text. Consistency in animations reinforces the video's style and makes it appear polished.

3. Controlling Animation Speed

Animation speed affects how viewers perceive the text. Slow animations create a relaxed feel, while faster animations give a sense of urgency or energy.

- **Timing with the Video Pace:**

  Match the animation speed with the overall pace of the video. For fast-paced content, use quicker animations, while slower-paced videos benefit from more gradual transitions.

- **Avoiding Excessive Motion:**

  Keep animations simple and avoid excessive bouncing or zooming effects. Overly animated text can make a video feel cluttered and chaotic, drawing focus away from the main content.

Adding Motion Graphics to Enhance Storytelling

Motion graphics are animated graphic elements that bring visual interest to videos, often used to illustrate complex information, highlight key points, or add aesthetic appeal. When used correctly, motion graphics enhance storytelling without overwhelming viewers.

1. Common Uses for Motion Graphics

Motion graphics can serve various purposes, from illustrating data to emphasizing important concepts. Here are some popular applications:

- **Data Visualization:**

  Motion graphics are excellent for presenting statistics, charts, or graphs, especially in educational or corporate videos. Animating these elements can make complex data more engaging and easier to understand.

- **Highlighting Key Points:**

  Use motion graphics to draw attention to essential points, such as summarizing information at the end of a section. This technique reinforces the message and helps viewers retain information.

- **Visualizing Processes or Concepts:**

  For instructional videos, motion graphics can depict processes step-by-step, providing a clear, visual representation. For instance, animated arrows or icons can illustrate a sequence of actions or guide viewers through steps.

2. Using Motion Graphics with Purpose

Motion graphics should add to the story, not just serve as decoration. When integrating motion graphics, consider their purpose in the context of the video:

- **Adding Context:**

  Use motion graphics to provide extra information that supports the main content, such as arrows indicating direction or icons representing objects.

- **Enhancing Visual Appeal without Distracting:** Motion graphics should enhance the visual appeal without becoming the main focus. Apply subtle motion and color to blend the graphics seamlessly with the video.

3. Tips for Effective Motion Graphics Design

Designing effective motion graphics requires thoughtful planning and consistency. Follow these best practices for a polished look:

- **Consistency in Style and Color:**

  Maintain a consistent style for all motion graphics, using the same colors, shapes, and animation types. Consistency helps create a cohesive look across the entire video.

- **Keeping It Simple:**

  Less is more when it comes to motion graphics. Avoid adding excessive elements, which can make the screen feel cluttered. Simple graphics are often more effective and easier for viewers to process.

- **Aligning with the Video's Tone:**

  Choose motion graphics that match the tone of your video. For instance, animated icons might suit a light-hearted tutorial, while sleek, minimalistic graphics work well for professional content.

Tips for Using Graphics to Reinforce Key Points Without Overwhelming Viewers

Graphics should reinforce the video's message without distracting or overwhelming the viewer. Here are some strategies to use graphics effectively:

1. Limit the Amount of On-Screen Text

Too much text on screen can distract from the visuals. Instead of filling the screen with information, summarize key points in a few words or short phrases.

- **Use Bullet Points Sparingly:**

  Bullet points are useful but should be limited to brief summaries. Aim for no more than three or four bullet points on screen at a time.

- **Highlighting Key Words:**

  Use bold text or color to highlight important words rather than displaying full sentences. This allows viewers to absorb the main idea without reading extensively.

2. Keep Graphics within Safe Margins

Ensure that all text and graphics stay within safe margins, especially if the video will be viewed on various screen sizes. Most editing software has guides or "safe zones" to help you keep elements from being cut off.

- **Avoiding Edge Clutter:**

- Leave some space around the edges of the screen. This improves readability and keeps the visuals from feeling cramped.

3. Use Visual Hierarchy for Emphasis

Visual hierarchy guides viewers' eyes, helping them focus on the most important elements first. By varying font sizes, weights, and colors, you can create a hierarchy that emphasizes critical information.

- **Larger Fonts for Titles and Headings:** Make the title or main point larger than secondary information, creating a clear hierarchy that guides viewers through the information naturally.

- **Contrast for Highlighting Key Information:** Using contrasting colors or font styles (such as bold or italic) on key points draws attention without requiring additional graphics or animations.

Incorporating text, titles, and graphics into a video enhances its visual appeal, readability, and professionalism. By mastering the use of titles, lower thirds, and credits, choosing readable fonts, applying animations with purpose, adding motion graphics to reinforce the story, and balancing visuals to avoid overwhelming viewers, you can elevate the quality of your videos.

These elements are not mere embellishments; they're tools that communicate with the viewer on both informational and emotional levels. With the skills from this chapter, you'll be able to design videos that are visually compelling, easy to follow, and polished—ensuring a positive, memorable experience for your audience.

CHAPTER 7

Advanced Editing Techniques for Professional Results

As you continue your journey into video editing, learning advanced techniques can significantly enhance the quality and appeal of your videos. These techniques add polish, creativity, and professionalism, making your content stand out. From adjusting the speed of footage to using green screen effects, multi-cam editing, and layering effects, each technique offers unique ways to transform your raw footage into a visually dynamic and engaging final product.

This chapter covers advanced editing techniques designed to take your skills to the next level. We'll explore speed adjustments, green screen (chroma key) editing, multi-cam editing, split screens, and layering effects and blending modes. By the end of this chapter, you'll have a range of powerful tools to make your videos more immersive, visually appealing, and professional.

Using Speed Adjustments (Slow-Motion, Time-Lapse, Reverse)

Speed adjustments are powerful techniques that allow you to manipulate time within your video. By speeding up, slowing down, or even reversing footage, you can add drama, emphasis, and visual interest to key moments.

1. Slow-Motion

Slow-motion is a technique where footage is played back at a slower-than-normal speed, creating a dramatic effect that can draw attention to specific actions, emotions, or details.

- **Creating Slow-Motion Footage:** To create slow-motion, shoot video at a higher frame rate (e.g., 60 fps or 120 fps) than the playback frame rate (usually 24 fps or 30 fps). This allows for smooth playback without the footage appearing choppy.

- **Using Slow-Motion for Impact:** Slow-motion is ideal for capturing impactful moments, such as a jump, an expression of emotion, or an object in motion. For example, in a sports video, you might use slow-motion to capture an athlete's movements in detail.

- **Adjusting Speed in Editing Software:**

  Most editing programs allow you to slow down footage by adjusting the speed settings. In Adobe Premiere Pro, for example, you can right-click on the clip and choose "Speed/Duration" to change the playback speed. Reducing speed to 50% or 25% creates a noticeable slow-motion effect.

2. Time-Lapse

Time-lapse is the opposite of slow-motion, where footage is sped up to show an event that occurs over a long period in a short amount of time. It's commonly used to show natural processes, like the movement of clouds, sunsets, or bustling city scenes.

- **Creating Time-Lapse Footage:**

  Time-lapse can be created by recording at a low frame rate or by speeding up normal footage during editing. Many cameras have a time-lapse setting, but you can also achieve this effect by increasing the speed of a regular clip.

- **Applications of Time-Lapse:**

  Use time-lapse to show changes over time, such as a flower blooming, a day transitioning into night, or a busy street scene. This effect is great for capturing the passage of time in a visually interesting way.

- **Speeding Up Footage in Editing Software:** To create a time-lapse effect, increase the speed of the clip in your editing software. For instance, in Final Cut Pro, you can set the speed to 500% or more to create a quick progression of time.

3. Reverse

Reversing footage is a creative effect where a clip is played backward, often used to create unique visual effects or add an unexpected twist.

- **Applications of Reverse Effect:**

  The reverse effect works well for certain actions, like a dropped item rising back up or someone walking backward. It can add a whimsical or surreal quality to your footage.

- **Applying Reverse Effect in Editing Software:**

Most editing programs allow you to reverse a clip with a single command. For instance, in DaVinci Resolve, you can right-click on the clip and select "Reverse Clip." Adjust the timing to make it appear natural within your scene.

Introduction to Green Screen (Chroma Key) Editing

Green screen, or chroma key, editing allows you to replace the background of a subject with any image or video, making it look like they're in a different environment. This technique is widely used in film production to create scenes that would be difficult or impossible to film otherwise.

1. Setting Up a Green Screen

Using a green screen requires shooting footage with a solid green (or blue) background. This background is then removed during editing and replaced with a different image or video.

- **Choosing the Right Background Color:**

  Green is commonly used because it contrasts with most skin tones and clothing. However, if your subject is wearing green, use a blue screen instead.

- **Lighting the Green Screen Evenly:**

  Proper lighting is essential to ensure that the green screen effect works smoothly. Even lighting reduces shadows and creates a uniform color, making it easier for the software to remove the background.

2. Removing the Green Screen (Chroma Keying)

Chroma keying is the process of selecting the green background and making it transparent in your editing software.

- **Using Chroma Key Tools:**

  Most editing software has a chroma key tool (e.g., Ultra Key in Premiere Pro, Keyer in Final Cut Pro). Select the green screen using this tool, and the software will make the color transparent, allowing you to place a new background behind the subject.

- **Adjusting Settings for Clean Edges:**

  Fine-tune the settings, such as "spill suppression" and "matte cleanup," to remove any green edges around the subject. Adjusting these controls will create a cleaner, more realistic look.

3. Choosing Replacement Backgrounds

Choose backgrounds that match the lighting and perspective of the original footage to create a seamless effect. For instance, if your subject was filmed under bright lighting, use a similarly lit background image to maintain consistency.

Mastering Multi-Cam Editing for Seamless Scene Switching

Multi-cam editing involves syncing footage from multiple cameras that captured the same scene from different angles. This technique is often used for interviews, live events, and dynamic scenes where multiple perspectives enhance the viewing experience.

1. Setting Up Multi-Cam Footage

To start, ensure all cameras are synchronized, either by using a clapboard (slate) or by syncing to audio.

- **Using a Clapboard or Audio Sync:**

   Clapboards create a visual and audio cue for each camera, making it easier to sync footage. If a clapboard isn't available, audio sync (matching the waveforms of each clip) works well.

- **Organizing Multi-Cam Clips in Editing Software:**
  Most editing software supports multi-cam
  sequences, allowing you to create a single timeline
  that includes all camera angles. Arrange each clip on
  a separate video track for easy access.

2. Editing Multi-Cam Sequences

Once set up, you can switch between camera angles in real-
time while playing back the footage, simulating a live editing
environment.

- **Switching Angles for Dynamic Cuts:**
  Switch angles based on the action or dialogue,
  focusing on the speaker in an interview or a wide shot
  for action scenes. Varying the angles keeps the video
  dynamic and visually interesting.

- **Matching Audio Across Clips:**
  Use a single audio track to maintain continuity,
  usually from the primary camera or an external
  recorder. This ensures consistent audio quality
  throughout the scene.

Creating Split Screens and Picture-in-Picture Effects

Split screens and picture-in-picture (PIP) effects display multiple video streams simultaneously, making them ideal for comparing scenes, showing different perspectives, or adding commentary.

1. Split Screens

Split screens divide the screen into multiple sections, each displaying a different video.

- **Arranging Clips for Balance:**

  Position clips side by side or in a grid, depending on the number of clips. For two clips, a vertical or horizontal split works well, while a grid layout is better for multiple clips.

- **Using Consistent Framing and Color Balance:** Ensure that each clip is framed similarly (e.g., close-up vs. wide shot) for a cohesive look. Consistent color grading across clips helps them appear uniform on screen.

2. Picture-in-Picture (PIP)

Picture-in-picture displays a smaller video within a larger one, commonly used for reaction videos or tutorials.

- **Positioning the PIP Window:**

  Place the smaller video in a corner, where it won't obstruct important content. Adjust its size to be visible but not distracting.

- **Applying Border or Drop Shadow:** Adding a thin border or shadow around the PIP window separates it from the background, making it easier to distinguish.

Layering Effects and Blending Modes for Creative Visuals

Layering effects and blending modes add texture, depth, and creativity to your footage. These techniques are often used in music videos, art films, and other projects that benefit from a stylized approach.

1. Layering Effects

Layering involves stacking multiple effects or clips to create a unique look.

- **Using Overlays:**

  Apply overlays like light leaks, grain, or textures to give footage a specific aesthetic. For example, light leaks add a vintage feel, while grain gives a filmic quality.

- **Adjusting Opacity for Subtle Effects:**

Reduce the opacity of overlays to blend them with the original footage. This softens the effect, making it less overpowering and more cohesive with the scene.

2. Applying Blending Modes

Blending modes determine how two layers interact, producing various effects by mixing pixels from each layer.

- **Popular Blending Modes:**

Common modes include "Screen" (for brightening effects), "Multiply" (for darkening), and "Overlay" (for contrast enhancement). Experiment with different modes to find one that enhances your footage.

- **Using Blending Modes for Texture and Light:** Apply blending modes with textures or light overlays to add depth and dimension. For instance, using the "Overlay" mode with a grunge texture adds a rugged, cinematic look.

Mastering advanced editing techniques elevates your video editing skills, allowing you to create dynamic, engaging, and visually stunning content. Techniques like speed adjustments, green screen editing, multi-cam sequences, split screens, and layering effects offer endless creative possibilities. By practicing these methods and experimenting with various styles, you'll enhance your ability to craft professional-quality videos that captivate audiences and leave a lasting impression.

CHAPTER 8

Exporting and Sharing Your Video

After the hard work of editing, refining, and perfecting your video, the final step is exporting and sharing it. While exporting may seem like a technical formality, it's a crucial part of the process. Export settings directly impact the video's quality, compatibility with platforms, and viewer experience. Additionally, sharing your video effectively can make a significant difference in its reach, engagement, and success.

This chapter explores the key aspects of exporting your video, from choosing the right settings for quality and file size to understanding formats, resolutions, and frame rates. We'll also cover how to optimize your video for social media, YouTube, and other online platforms, create eye-catching thumbnails and titles, and employ strategies to share your work confidently and build an audience.

Choosing the Right Export Settings for Quality and File Size

Selecting the appropriate export settings is essential for achieving high-quality visuals without creating excessively large files. The goal is to balance quality and file size to ensure smooth playback and faster upload times. Here's a breakdown of the main export settings you should understand:

1. Resolution

Resolution is the number of pixels in each frame, usually measured in width x height (e.g., 1920 x 1080). Higher resolutions provide better clarity and detail but also result in larger file sizes.

- **Common Resolutions:**

1080p (1920 x 1080): Full HD, standard for most online platforms.

4K (3840 x 2160): Ultra HD, often used for high-quality YouTube videos, streaming, and television.

720p (1280 x 720): HD, acceptable for smaller screens and faster uploads but not ideal for professional content.

- **Choosing the Right Resolution:** Consider your audience and platform. For YouTube and most social media, 1080p is sufficient, while 4K may be appropriate for cinematic projects or if you anticipate viewers using large screens.

2. Frame Rate

The frame rate, measured in frames per second (fps), determines how smoothly motion appears in the video. Common frame rates include:

- **24 fps:** The standard for cinematic content, providing a natural, film-like quality.

- **30 fps:** Common for online videos and social media, offering smooth playback without a "cinematic" look.

- **60 fps:** Used for high-action content like sports or gaming, as it captures more detail in fast-moving scenes.

- **Choosing the Right Frame Rate:** Match the frame rate of your original footage or the platform's preferred frame rate. YouTube supports a variety of frame rates, but 24 or 30 fps is usually ideal for general content.

3. Bitrate

Bitrate controls the amount of data used to store each second of video, directly impacting quality and file size. Higher bitrates increase quality but also result in larger files.

- **Constant vs. Variable Bitrate:**

Constant Bitrate (CBR): Delivers a consistent quality throughout, often resulting in larger files.

Variable Bitrate (VBR): Adjusts bitrate based on scene complexity, optimizing quality without excessively large files.

- **Recommended   Bitrates:** For 1080p videos, 8-12 Mbps is usually adequate. For 4K, 35-45 Mbps ensures high quality without excessive size. Use VBR to strike a balance between quality and file size.

4. Audio Settings

Audio settings are often overlooked but equally important. Ensure high audio quality by setting a sample rate of 48 kHz and a bitrate of at least 128 kbps.

- **Audio Format:** Use AAC (Advanced Audio Codec) for compatibility with most platforms.

- **Bitrate Recommendation:**

128 kbps is standard for voice-over content, while 192-320 kbps is ideal for videos where music or sound effects play a prominent role.

These export settings impact your final file size and playback quality. Experiment with different settings to find a balance that meets your needs without sacrificing quality.

Understanding Formats, Resolutions, and Frame Rates for Different Platforms

Each platform has its own requirements and best practices for video uploads. Choosing the right format, resolution, and frame rate helps ensure compatibility, efficient uploads, and optimal viewing experiences for your audience.

1. Common Video Formats

Different formats offer various levels of compression, compatibility, and quality. The most widely accepted format is MP4 (H.264 codec), as it maintains high quality with relatively small file sizes.

- **MP4 (H.264):** Most commonly used format for online platforms. It provides a good balance of quality and file size.

- **MOV:** Offers higher quality and is compatible with most platforms, but files are often larger.

- **AVI:** A high-quality format, but it produces large files and is less compatible with online platforms.

For most cases, MP4 is recommended as it works well with YouTube, Instagram, Facebook, and other popular platforms.

2. Platform-Specific Resolutions and Aspect Ratios

Platforms vary in their preferred resolutions and aspect ratios, which influence how your video appears on screens.

- **YouTube:**

Resolution: 1080p or 4K (16:9 aspect ratio)

Frame rate: 24, 30, or 60 fps

- **Instagram:**

Stories and IGTV: 1080 x 1920 (vertical, 9:16 aspect ratio)

Feed: 1080 x 1080 (square, 1:1) or 1080 x 1350 (4:5 aspect ratio)

- **Facebook:**

Resolution: 1080p (16:9 for landscape or 1:1 for square)

Frame rate: 24 or 30 fps

Selecting the appropriate resolution and aspect ratio for each platform improves the video's appearance and accessibility for viewers.

3. Frame Rates for Different Platforms

While most platforms support multiple frame rates, the choice depends on the style of your content:

- **24 fps:** Suitable for cinematic or storytelling videos, as it creates a film-like effect.

- **30 fps:** Standard for most online content, providing smooth playback.

- **60 fps:** Recommended for high-motion content, including sports or gaming.

Exporting for Social Media, YouTube, and Other Online Platforms

Exporting specifically for online platforms involves understanding each platform's technical requirements and best practices.

1. Exporting for YouTube

YouTube supports various resolutions and frame rates, making it a versatile platform for all types of content.

Recommended Settings:

Format: MP4 (H.264 codec)

Resolution: 1080p or 4K

Frame rate: 24, 30, or 60 fps

Bitrate: 8-12 Mbps for 1080p, 35-45 Mbps for 4K

YouTube also automatically adjusts your video's resolution for different devices, so ensure your settings are optimized for high quality.

2. Exporting for Instagram

Instagram's format and aspect ratio requirements differ between Stories, Feed, and IGTV, so export each video with the specific aspect ratio in mind.

- **Feed Videos:** 1:1 or 4:5 aspect ratio, 1080 x 1080 or 1080 x 1350 resolution.

- **Stories and IGTV:** 9:16 aspect ratio, 1080 x 1920 resolution.

Instagram videos are typically short, so file size is less of a concern, but quality and aspect ratio are key.

3. Exporting for Facebook

Facebook supports various video formats but generally favors square or horizontal videos for News Feed and vertical videos for Stories.

Recommended Settings:

Format: MP4 (H.264 codec)

Resolution: 1080p (16:9 for landscape or 1:1 for square)

Frame rate: 24 or 30 fps

Tips for Creating Thumbnails and Titles that Attract Viewers

Creating an appealing thumbnail and title is crucial for grabbing viewers' attention and encouraging them to click on your video.

1. Designing Eye-Catching Thumbnails

Thumbnails serve as the first impression of your video. They should be visually appealing, informative, and relevant.

- **Using Bright Colors and High Contrast:** Bright colors stand out against the background, attracting more attention. Use contrasting colors to make text and images pop.

- **Including Faces and Emotions:**

  Thumbnails with faces, especially showing emotions, are more engaging and relatable, drawing viewers in.

- **Adding Bold Text:**

  Include brief, bold text to convey the video's main theme. Keep it short and easy to read, as thumbnails are often viewed on small screens.

2. Crafting Compelling Titles

A great title entices viewers to watch and provides context about the video's content.

- **Using Keywords for Search Optimization:**

  Include keywords relevant to your topic to improve searchability. This helps your video appear in relevant search results.

- **Creating Curiosity or Providing Value:**

  Titles that hint at a benefit (e.g., "How to Edit Videos Like a Pro") or create curiosity (e.g., "The Secret to

Perfect Sound in Videos") are more likely to attract clicks.

Strategies for Building an Audience and Sharing Your Work Confidently

Sharing your video and building an audience requires a strategic approach. Here are effective strategies to expand your reach and connect with viewers.

1. Consistency in Posting

Regular posting builds viewer expectations and keeps your content fresh in their minds.

- **Setting a Posting Schedule:**

  Commit to a schedule, such as posting every week, to maintain consistency and build momentum.

2. Engaging with Viewers

Building an audience involves creating a community, not just posting videos.

- **Responding to Comments:**

  Engaging with viewers in the comments section builds relationships and encourages return viewers.

3. Leveraging Multiple Platforms

Promote your video across various social media channels to increase its visibility.

- **Cross-Promoting Content:**

  Share short clips or teasers on Instagram, Facebook, and Twitter to drive traffic to the full video.

4. Using Analytics to Improve

Most platforms provide analytics that offer insights into viewer behavior, including watch time, demographics, and engagement.

- **Analyzing Viewer Retention:**

  Monitor which parts of your video hold viewers' attention and adjust future content to maintain engagement.

Exporting and sharing your video effectively is the final step in producing professional, engaging content. By selecting the right export settings, understanding platform requirements, designing attractive thumbnails and titles, and implementing audience-building strategies, you can maximize the reach and impact of your video.

Mastering these techniques not only enhances the technical quality of your content but also positions it for greater visibility and engagement, helping you to confidently share your work and build a loyal audience. With these final touches, your video editing journey comes full circle, empowering you to deliver polished, high-quality videos that resonate with viewers across platforms.

CONCLUSION

Bringing Your Vision to Life

As you reach the conclusion of *Guide to Video Editing Techniques*, you have walked through a comprehensive journey of learning and mastering the essential skills needed to create engaging, professional, and visually captivating videos. From understanding the basics to diving into advanced techniques, you've gained a wealth of knowledge on how to transform raw footage into polished content that can entertain, inform, or inspire an audience.

Video editing is both an art and a science, requiring technical skills, creativity, and a keen understanding of storytelling. With each chapter, we've explored various facets of video editing—from foundational concepts like cutting and trimming footage to advanced skills like color grading, multi-cam editing, and green screen effects. Each technique is a tool in your editing arsenal, empowering you to convey stories, express emotions, and capture attention effectively.

The world of video editing is dynamic, evolving rapidly with technological advancements and changing viewer preferences. Today, video content is more accessible and diverse than ever before. Platforms like YouTube, Instagram,

TikTok, and streaming services have reshaped how people consume media, making it essential for editors to produce high-quality, engaging content that stands out amidst an endless stream of videos. This concluding chapter serves as a reflective summary of your learning and a motivational guide as you embark on your journey as a video editor.

Embracing the Art of Storytelling

At the heart of every video lies a story—whether it's a vlog, a documentary, a commercial, or a cinematic piece. Storytelling is a timeless element that resonates universally, engaging audiences by taking them on a journey or conveying a message. As a video editor, you are not simply piecing together clips; you are crafting a narrative that connects with viewers on an emotional level. Through thoughtful editing choices, you control the pacing, emphasize key moments, and guide your audience's experience.

Throughout this book, you've learned how essential elements like timing, transitions, and music can elevate a video from a collection of clips to a compelling narrative. The art of storytelling goes beyond technical skills; it requires empathy, creativity, and an understanding of human emotions. Whether you're working on a short video or a feature-length project, remember that each editing decision should serve the story. As you develop your skills further, you'll discover how to subtly influence how your audience feels and reacts to your work.

The Power of Creativity and Experimentation

Video editing offers endless possibilities for creativity. From experimenting with different effects and transitions to trying out unique color grades and blending modes, each project is an opportunity to push the boundaries of your creativity. Advanced techniques like speed adjustments, split screens, and green screen effects allow you to add a personal touch, creating videos that stand out and reflect your unique style.

Experimentation is an essential part of becoming a skilled editor. Each project you work on presents new challenges and learning opportunities. Don't be afraid to take risks, try unconventional edits, or play with new techniques. Video editing software offers a sandbox for innovation, where you can test your ideas without limitations. By continually exploring new tools and effects, you can refine your style and develop a signature approach that makes your work recognizably yours.

Technical Mastery for Consistent Quality

While creativity is vital, technical expertise ensures that your videos maintain a professional standard. High-quality videos require precise attention to detail—from color correction to audio balancing and export settings. As a video editor, you are responsible for delivering content that not only tells a story but also meets the quality expectations of viewers, clients, or employers.

Mastering technical skills is a process that grows with experience. Understanding file formats, resolutions, and frame rates ensures that your videos are optimized for their intended platforms, whether that's social media, streaming, or television. Additionally, the ability to clean up audio, apply noise reduction, and adjust bitrate settings can make a significant difference in the viewer's experience.

Investing time in perfecting your technical skills allows you to work efficiently and confidently across various types of projects. By building a strong technical foundation, you are equipped to tackle more complex projects and ensure consistent quality in your work, no matter the content or platform.

Adapting to a Changing Media Landscape

The video editing industry is continuously evolving, driven by advancements in technology and changing audience preferences. New tools, software updates, and editing techniques regularly emerge, offering editors new ways to enhance their work. Staying current with industry trends, learning new software features, and experimenting with emerging techniques are all part of being a modern video editor.

The popularity of short-form video content on platforms like Instagram Reels and TikTok has introduced unique editing styles that emphasize quick cuts, dynamic effects, and creative transitions. While long-form content remains essential for many types of storytelling, adapting to these new formats can expand your versatility and open up new opportunities. Embrace the constant change in the industry as a way to grow, refine your skills, and stay relevant.

Building an Audience and Sharing Your Work

Video editing doesn't end with exporting a finished product. Sharing your work effectively is just as important as the editing process itself. Building an audience requires understanding how to present your videos in ways that attract viewers and encourage engagement. Creating appealing thumbnails, writing compelling titles, and choosing appropriate distribution channels are all integral parts of reaching your intended audience.

In today's digital landscape, social media offers powerful tools for promoting your work, connecting with other creators, and receiving feedback. Platforms like YouTube, Vimeo, and Instagram allow you to showcase your skills, gain exposure, and potentially attract clients or collaborators. Sharing your work and receiving feedback is essential for growth, providing insights that help you understand what resonates with audiences and what areas need improvement.

Continuing Your Journey as an Editor

Becoming a skilled video editor is a journey that doesn't end with this book. Each project you complete, every skill you acquire, and each new technique you try contributes to your growth as an editor. The most successful editors are lifelong learners who continually refine their skills, stay curious, and adapt to new challenges.

As you move forward, continue seeking inspiration from other creators, studying films, and exploring online resources. Take time to analyze the work of professional editors, deconstructing their choices and learning from their styles. You may also consider taking online courses, joining communities, or attending workshops to stay engaged and expand your network.

Final Thoughts: A Personal Journey

Video editing is as much a personal journey as it is a technical skill. It's a craft that allows you to express your creativity, shape powerful stories, and leave a lasting impact on viewers. Every edit you make, every scene you cut, and every effect you add contributes to your unique storytelling voice. Whether you're editing videos for personal projects, clients, or an audience of millions, each piece of content you create is an opportunity to learn, grow, and connect.

This book has given you the tools and knowledge to approach video editing with confidence, precision, and creativity. Now, it's up to you to continue practicing, experimenting, and evolving your craft. Remember, every successful editor started as a beginner, and every great project begins with a single clip on a timeline.

In the world of video editing, there are no limits to what you can achieve. With determination, curiosity, and the willingness to keep learning, you'll discover endless possibilities to bring your ideas to life. So go ahead—tell your stories, experiment with techniques, and share your work with the world. Your journey as a video editor is just beginning, and the potential for what you can create is limitless.

www.ingramcontent.com/pod-product-compliance
Lightning Source LLC
Chambersburg PA
CBHW071518220526
45472CB00003B/1069